P9-BIH-491

CHABOT COLLEGE-HAY
2 555 000 047785 5

Also by Athol Fugard

Plays

Boesman & Lena & Other Plays

Dimetos & Two Early Plays

Statements: Three Plays

Sizwe Bansi Is Dead & The Island

A Lesson from Aloes

Novel

Tsotsi

Film Scripts

The Guest

Marigolds in August

"MASTER HAROLD"

. . . and the boys

MARTHA SWOPE

"MASTER HAROLD"

...and the boys

Athol Fugard

Alfred A. Knopf   New York   1982 

THIS IS A BORZOI BOOK
PUBLISHED BY ALFRED A. KNOPF, INC.

 Published in the United States by Alfred A. Knopf, Inc., New York, and simultaneously in Canada by Random House of Canada Limited, Toronto. Distributed by Random House, Inc., New York.

Originally produced in 1982 by The Yale Repertory Theatre, New Haven, Connecticut.

Originally produced on Broadway by The Schubert Organization, Freydberg/Bloch Productions, Dasha Epstein, Emanuel Azenberg and David Geffen.

Library of Congress Cataloging in Publication Data
Fugard, Athol.
"Master Harold"—and the boys.
"A Borzoi book."
1. South Africa—Social life and customs—Drama.
I. Title.
PR9369.3.F8M3 1982 822 82-48027
ISBN 0-394-52874-3 AACR2

Manufactured in the United States of America
FIRST EDITION

for Sam and H.D.F.

The first performance of

"MASTER HAROLD"
. . . *and the boys*

was given at the Yale Repertory Theatre on March 12, 1982, with the following cast:

HALLY	Željko Ivanek
SAM	Zakes Mokae
WILLIE	Danny Glover

The production was directed by the author.
Sets were designed by Jane Clark.
Costumes were designed by Sheila McLamb.
Lights were designed by David Noling.

In New York, the role of Hally was played by Lonny Price.

"MASTER HAROLD"

...and the boys

The St. George's Park Tea Room on a wet and windy Port Elizabeth afternoon.

Tables and chairs have been cleared and are stacked on one side except for one which stands apart with a single chair. On this table a knife, fork, spoon and side plate in anticipation of a simple meal, together with a pile of comic books.

Other elements: a serving counter with a few stale cakes under glass and a not very impressive display of sweets, cigarettes and cool drinks, etc.; a few cardboard advertising handouts—Cadbury's Chocolate, Coca-Cola—and a blackboard on which an untrained hand has chalked up the prices of Tea, Coffee, Scones, Milkshakes—all flavors—and Cool Drinks; a few sad ferns in pots; a telephone; an old-style jukebox.

There is an entrance on one side and an exit into a kitchen on the other.

Leaning on the solitary table, his head cupped in one hand as he pages through one of the comic books, is SAM. A black man in his mid-forties. He wears the white coat of a waiter. Behind him on his knees, mopping down the floor with a bucket of water and a rag, is WILLIE. Also black and about the same age as Sam. He has his sleeves and trousers rolled up.

The year: 1950

WILLIE (*Singing as he works*)
"She was scandalizin' my name,
She took my money
She called me honey
But she was scandalizin' my name.
Called it love but was playin' a game . . ."

(*He gets up and moves the bucket. Stands thinking for a moment, then, raising his arms to hold an imaginary partner, he launches into an intricate ballroom dance step. Although a mildly comic figure, he reveals a reasonable degree of accomplishment*)

Hey, Sam.

(SAM, *absorbed in the comic book, does not respond*)

Hey, Boet Sam!

(SAM *looks up*)

I'm getting it. The quickstep. Look now and tell me. (*He repeats the step*) Well?

SAM (*Encouragingly*) Show me again.

WILLIE Okay, count for me.

SAM Ready?

WILLIE Ready.

SAM Five, six, seven, eight . . . (WILLIE *starts to dance*) A-n-d one two three four . . . and one two three four. . . . (*Ad libbing as* WILLIE *dances*) Your shoulders, Willie . . . your shoulders! Don't look down! Look happy, Willie! Relax, Willie!

WILLIE (*Desperate but still dancing*) I am relax.

SAM No, you're not.

WILLIE (*He falters*) Ag no man, Sam! Mustn't talk. You make me make mistakes.

SAM But you're too stiff.

WILLIE Yesterday I'm not straight . . . today I'm too stiff!

SAM Well, you are. You asked me and I'm telling you.

WILLIE Where?

SAM Everywhere. Try to glide through it.

WILLIE Glide?

SAM Ja, make it smooth. And give it more style. It must look like you're enjoying yourself.

WILLIE (*Emphatically*) I wasn't.

SAM Exactly.

WILLIE How can I enjoy myself? Not straight, too stiff and now it's also glide, give it more style, make it smooth. . . . Haai! Is hard to remember all those things, Boet Sam.

SAM That's your trouble. You're trying too hard.

WILLIE I try hard because it *is* hard.

SAM But don't let me see it. The secret is to make it look easy. Ballroom must look happy, Willie, not like hard work. It must . . . Ja! . . . it must look like romance.

WILLIE Now another one! What's romance?

SAM Love story with happy ending. A handsome man in tails, and in his arms, smiling at him, a beautiful lady in evening dress!

WILLIE Fred Astaire, Ginger Rogers.

SAM You got it. Tapdance or ballroom, it's the same. Romance. In two weeks' time when the judges look at you and Hilda, they must see a man and a woman who are dancing their way to a happy ending. What I saw was you holding her like you were frightened she was going to run away.

WILLIE Ja! Because that is what she wants to do! I got no romance left for Hilda anymore, Boet Sam.

SAM Then pretend. When you put your arms around Hilda, imagine she is Ginger Rogers.

WILLIE With no teeth? You try.

SAM Well, just remember, there's only two weeks left.

WILLIE I know, I know! (*To the jukebox*) I do it better with music. You got sixpence for Sarah Vaughan?

SAM That's a slow foxtrot. You're practicing the quick-step.

WILLIE I'll practice slow foxtrot.

SAM (*Shaking his head*) It's your turn to put money in the jukebox.

WILLIE I only got bus fare to go home. (*He returns disconsolately to his work*) Love story and happy ending! She's doing it all right, Boet Sam, but is not me she's giving happy endings. Fuckin' whore! Three nights now she doesn't come practice. I wind up gramophone, I get record ready and I sit and wait. What happens? Nothing. Ten o'clock I start dancing with my pillow. You try and practice romance by yourself, Boet Sam. Struesgod, she doesn't come tonight I take back my dress and ballroom shoes and I find me new partner. Size twenty-six. Shoes size seven. And now she's also making trouble for me with the baby again. Reports me to Child Wellfed, that I'm not giving her money. She lies! Every week I am giving her money for milk. And how do I know is my baby? Only his hair looks like me. She's fucking around all the time I turn my back. Hilda Samuels is a bitch! (*Pause*) Hey, Sam!

SAM Ja.

WILLIE You listening?

SAM Ja.

WILLIE So what you say?

SAM About Hilda?

WILLIE Ja.

SAM When did you last give her a hiding?

WILLIE (*Reluctantly*) Sunday night.

SAM And today is Thursday.

WILLIE (*He knows what's coming*) Okay.

SAM Hiding on Sunday night, then Monday, Tuesday and Wednesday she doesn't come to practice . . . and you are asking me why?

WILLIE I said okay, Boet Sam!

SAM You hit her too much. One day she's going to leave you for good.

WILLIE So? She makes me the hell-in too much.

SAM (*Emphasizing his point*) *Too* much and *too* hard. You had the same trouble with Eunice.

WILLIE Because she also make the hell-in, Boet Sam. She never got the steps right. Even the waltz.

SAM Beating her up every time she makes a mistake in the waltz? (*Shaking his head*) No, Willie! That takes the pleasure out of ballroom dancing.

WILLIE Hilda is not too bad with the waltz, Boet Sam. Is the quickstep where the trouble starts.

SAM (*Teasing him gently*) How's your pillow with the quickstep?

WILLIE (*Ignoring the tease*) Good! And why? Because it got no legs. That's her trouble. She can't move them quick enough, Boet Sam. I start the record and before halfway Count Basie is already winning. Only time we catch up with him is when gramophone runs down.

(SAM *laughs*)

Haaikona, Boet Sam, is not funny.

SAM (*Snapping his fingers*) I got it! Give her a handicap.

WILLIE What's that?

SAM Give her a ten-second start and then let Count Basie go. Then I put my money on her. Hot favorite in the Ballroom Stakes: Hilda Samuels ridden by Willie Malopo.

WILLIE (*Turning away*) I'm not talking to you no more.

SAM (*Relenting*) Sorry, Willie . . .

WILLIE It's finish between us.

SAM Okay, okay . . . I'll stop.

WILLIE You can also fuck off.

SAM Willie, listen! I want to help you!

WILLIE No more jokes?

SAM I promise.

WILLIE Okay. Help me.

SAM (*His turn to hold an imaginary partner*) Look and learn. Feet together. Back straight. Body relaxed. Right hand placed gently in the small of her back and wait for the music. Don't start worrying about making mistakes or the judges or the other competitors. It's just you, Hilda and the music, and you're going to have a good time. What Count Basie do you play?

WILLIE "You the cream in my coffee, you the salt in my stew."

SAM Right. Give it to me in strict tempo.

WILLIE Ready?

SAM Ready.

WILLIE A-n-d . . . (*Singing*) Start here!

"You the cream in my coffee.
You the salt in my stew.
You will always be my
necessity.
I'd be lost without
you. . . ." (*etc.*)

(SAM *launches into the quickstep. He is obviously a much more accomplished dancer than* WILLIE. HALLY *enters. A seventeen-year-old white boy. Wet raincoat and school case. He stops and watches* SAM. *The demonstration comes to an end with a flourish. Applause from* HALLY *and* WILLIE)

HALLY Bravo! No question about it. First place goes to Mr. Sam Semela.

WILLIE (*In total agreement*) You was gliding with style, Boet Sam.

HALLY (*Cheerfully*) How's it, chaps?

SAM Okay, Hally.

WILLIE (*Springing to attention like a soldier and saluting*) At your service, Master Harold!

HALLY Not long to the big event, hey!

SAM Two weeks.

HALLY You nervous?

SAM No.

HALLY Think you stand a chance?

SAM Let's just say I'm ready to go out there and dance.

HALLY It looked like it. What about you, Willie?

(WILLIE *groans*)

What's the matter?

SAM He's got leg trouble.

HALLY (*Innocently*) Oh, sorry to hear that, Willie.

WILLIE Boet Sam! You promised. (WILLIE *returns to his work*)

(HALLY *deposits his school case and takes off his raincoat. His clothes are a little neglected and untidy: black blazer with school badge, gray flannel trousers in need of an ironing, khaki shirt and tie, black shoes.* SAM *has fetched a towel for* HALLY *to dry his hair*)

HALLY God, what a lousy bloody day. It's coming down cats and dogs out there. Bad for business, chaps . . . (*Conspiratorial whisper*) . . . but it also means we're in for a nice quiet afternoon.

SAM You can speak loud. Your Mom's not here.

HALLY Out shopping?

SAM No. The hospital.

HALLY But it's Thursday. There's no visiting on Thursday afternoons. Is my Dad okay?

SAM Sounds like it. In fact, I think he's going home.

HALLY (*Stopped short by* SAM's *remark*) What do you mean?

SAM The hospital phoned.

HALLY To say what?

SAM I don't know. I just heard your Mom talking.

HALLY So what makes you say he's going home?

SAM It sounded as if they were telling her to come and fetch him.

(HALLY *thinks about what* SAM *has said for a few seconds*)

HALLY When did she leave?

SAM About an hour ago. She said she would phone you. Want to eat?

(HALLY *doesn't respond*)

Hally, want your lunch?

HALLY I suppose so. (*His mood has changed*) What's on the menu? . . . as if I don't know.

SAM Soup, followed by meat pie and gravy.

HALLY Today's?

SAM No.

HALLY And the soup?

SAM Nourishing pea soup.

HALLY Just the soup. (*The pile of comic books on the table*) And these?

SAM For your Dad. Mr. Kempston brought them.

HALLY You haven't been reading them, have you?

SAM Just looking.

HALLY (*Examining the comics*) *Jungle Jim . . . Batman and Robin . . . Tarzan* . . . God, what rubbish! Mental pollution. Take them away.

(SAM *exits waltzing into the kitchen.* HALLY *turns to* WILLIE)

HALLY Did you hear my Mom talking on the telephone, Willie?

WILLIE No, Master Hally. I was at the back.

HALLY And she didn't say anything to you before she left?

WILLIE She said I must clean the floors.

HALLY I mean about my Dad.

WILLIE She didn't say nothing to me about him, Master Hally.

HALLY (*With conviction*) No! It can't be. They said he needed at least another three weeks of treatment. Sam's definitely made a mistake. (*Rummages through his school case, finds a book and settles down at the table to read*) So, Willie!

WILLIE Yes, Master Hally! Schooling okay today?

HALLY Yes, okay. . . . (*He thinks about it*) . . . No, not really. Ag, what's the difference? I don't care. And Sam says you've got problems.

WILLIE Big problems.

HALLY Which leg is sore?

(WILLIE *groans*)

Both legs.

WILLIE There is nothing wrong with my legs. Sam is just making jokes.

HALLY So then you *will* be in the competition.

WILLIE Only if I can find me a partner.

HALLY But what about Hilda?

SAM (*Returning with a bowl of soup*) She's the one who's got trouble with her legs.

HALLY What sort of trouble, Willie?

SAM From the way he describes it, I think the lady has gone a bit lame.

HALLY Good God! Have you taken her to see a doctor?

SAM I think a vet would be better.

HALLY What do you mean?

SAM What do you call it again when a racehorse goes very fast?

HALLY Gallop?

SAM That's it!

WILLIE Boet Sam!

HALLY "A gallop down the homestretch to the winning post." But what's that got to do with Hilda?

SAM Count Basie always gets there first.

(WILLIE *lets fly with his slop rag. It misses* SAM *and hits* HALLY)

HALLY (*Furious*) For Christ's sake, Willie! What the hell do you think you're doing!

WILLIE Sorry, Master Hally, but it's him. . . .

HALLY Act your bloody age! (*Hurls the rag back at* WILLIE) Cut out the nonsense now and get on with your work. And you too, Sam. Stop fooling around.

(SAM *moves away*)

No. Hang on. I haven't finished! Tell me exactly what my Mom said.

SAM I have. "When Hally comes, tell him I've gone to the hospital and I'll phone him."

HALLY She didn't say anything about taking my Dad home?

SAM No. It's just that when she was talking on the phone . . .

HALLY (*Interrupting him*) No, Sam. They can't be discharging him. She would have said so if they were. In any case, we saw him last night and he wasn't in good shape at all. Staff nurse even said there was talk about taking more X-rays. And now suddenly today he's better? If anything, it sounds more like a bad turn to me . . . which I sincerely hope it isn't. Hang on . . . how long ago did you say she left?

SAM Just before two . . . (*His wrist watch*) . . . hour and a half.

HALLY I know how to settle it. (*Behind the counter to the telephone. Talking as he dials*) Let's give her ten minutes to get to the hospital, ten minutes to load him up, another ten, at the most, to get home and another ten to get him inside. Forty minutes. They should have been home for at least half an hour already. (*Pause—he waits with the receiver to his ear*) No reply, chaps. And you know why? Because she's at his bedside in hospital helping him pull through a bad turn. You definitely heard wrong.

SAM Okay.

(*As far as* HALLY *is concerned, the matter is settled. He returns to his table, sits down and divides his attention between the book and his soup.* SAM *is at his school case and picks up a textbook*)

Modern Graded Mathematics for Standards Nine and Ten. (*Opens it at random and laughs at something he sees*) Who is this supposed to be?

HALLY Old fart-face Prentice.

SAM Teacher?

HALLY Thinks he is. And believe me, that is not a bad likeness.

SAM Has he seen it?

HALLY Yes.

SAM What did he say?

HALLY Tried to be clever, as usual. Said I was no Leonardo da Vinci and that bad art had to be punished. So, six of the best, and his are bloody good.

SAM On your bum?

HALLY Where else? The days when I got them on my hands are gone forever, Sam.

SAM With your trousers down!

HALLY No. He's not quite that barbaric.

SAM That's the way they do it in jail.

HALLY (*Flicker of morbid interest*) Really?

SAM Ja. When the magistrate sentences you to "strokes with a light cane."

HALLY Go on.

SAM They make you lie down on a bench. One policeman pulls down your trousers and holds your ankles, another one pulls your shirt over your head and holds your arms . . .

HALLY Thank you! That's enough.

SAM . . . and the one that gives you the strokes talks to you gently and for a long time between each one. (*He laughs*)

HALLY I've heard enough, Sam! Jesus! It's a bloody awful world when you come to think of it. People can be real bastards.

SAM That's the way it is, Hally.

HALLY It doesn't *have* to be that way. There is something called progress, you know. We don't exactly burn people at the stake anymore.

SAM Like Joan of Arc.

HALLY Correct. If she was captured today, she'd be given a fair trial.

SAM And then the death sentence.

HALLY (*A world-weary sigh*) I know, I know! I oscillate between hope and despair for this world as well, Sam. But things will change, you wait and see. One day somebody is going to get up and give history a kick up the backside and get it going again.

SAM Like who?

HALLY (*After thought*) They're called social reformers. Every age, Sam, has got its social reformer. My history book is full of them.

SAM So where's ours?

HALLY Good question. And I hate to say it, but the answer is: I don't know. Maybe he hasn't even been born yet. Or is still only a babe in arms at his mother's breast. God, what a thought.

SAM So we just go on waiting.

HALLY Ja, looks like it. (*Back to his soup and the book*)

SAM (*Reading from the textbook*) "Introduction: In some mathematical problems only the magnitude . . ." (*He mispronounces the word "magnitude"*)

HALLY (*Correcting him without looking up*) Magnitude.

SAM What's it mean?

HALLY How big it is. The size of the thing.

SAM (*Reading*) ". . . magnitude of the quantities is of importance. In other problems we need to know whether these quantities are negative or positive. For example, whether there is a debit or credit bank balance . . ."

HALLY Whether you're broke or not.

SAM ". . . whether the temperature is above or below Zero . . ."

HALLY Naught degrees. Cheerful state of affairs! No cash and you're freezing to death. Mathematics won't get you out of that one.

SAM "All these quantities are called . . ." (*Spelling the word*) . . . s-c-a-l . . .

HALLY Scalars.

SAM Scalars! (*Shaking his head with a laugh*) You understand all that?

HALLY (*Turning a page*) No. And I don't intend to try.

SAM So what happens when the exams come?

HALLY Failing a maths exam isn't the end of the world, Sam. How many times have I told you that examination results don't measure intelligence?

SAM I would say about as many times as you've failed one of them.

HALLY (*Mirthlessly*) Ha, ha, ha.

SAM (*Simultaneously*) Ha, ha, ha.

HALLY Just remember Winston Churchill didn't do particularly well at school.

SAM You've also told me that one many times.

HALLY Well, it just so happens to be the truth.

SAM (*Enjoying the word*) Magnitude! Magnitude! Show me how to use it.

HALLY (*After thought*) An intrepid social reformer will not be daunted by the magnitude of the task he has undertaken.

SAM (*Impressed*) Couple of jaw-breakers in there!

HALLY I gave you three for the price of one. Intrepid, daunted and magnitude. I did that once in an exam. Put five of the words I had to explain in one sentence. It was half a page long.

SAM Well, I'll put my money on you in the English exam.

HALLY Piece of cake. Eighty percent without even trying.

SAM (*Another textbook from* HALLY'S *case*) And history?

HALLY So-so. I'll scrape through. In the fifties if I'm lucky.

SAM You didn't do too badly last year.

HALLY Because we had World War One. That at least had some action. You try to find that in the South African Parliamentary system.

SAM (*Reading from the history textbook*) "Napoleon and the principle of equality." Hey! This sounds interesting. "After concluding peace with Britain in 1802, Napoleon used a brief period of calm to in-sti-tute . . ."

HALLY Introduce.

SAM ". . . many reforms. Napoleon regarded all people as equal before the law and wanted them to have equal opportunities for advancement. All ves-ti-ges of the feu-dal system with its oppression of the poor were abolished." Vestiges, feudal system and abolished. I'm all right on oppression.

HALLY I'm thinking. He swept away . . . abolished . . . the last remains . . . vestiges . . . of the bad old days . . . feudal system.

SAM Ha! There's the social reformer we're waiting for. He sounds like a man of some magnitude.

HALLY I'm not so sure about that. It's a damn good title for a book, though. A man of magnitude!

SAM He sounds pretty big to me, Hally.

HALLY Don't confuse historical significance with greatness. But maybe I'm being a bit prejudiced. Have a look in there and you'll see he's two chapters long. And hell! . . . has he only got dates, Sam, all of which you've got to remember! This campaign and that campaign, and then, because of all the fighting, the next thing is we get Peace Treaties all over the place. And what's the end of the story? Battle of Waterloo, which he loses. Wasn't worth it. No, I don't know about him as a man of magnitude.

SAM Then who would you say was?

HALLY To answer that, we need a definition of greatness, and I suppose that would be somebody who . . . somebody who benefited all mankind.

SAM Right. But like who?

HALLY (*He speaks with total conviction*) Charles Darwin. Remember him? That big book from the library. *The Origin of the Species.*

SAM Him?

HALLY Yes. For his Theory of Evolution.

SAM You didn't finish it.

HALLY I ran out of time. I didn't finish it because my two weeks was up. But I'm going to take it out again after I've digested what I read. It's safe. I've hidden it away in the Theology section. Nobody ever goes in there. And anyway who are you to talk? You hardly even looked at it.

SAM I tried. I looked at the chapters in the beginning and I saw one called "The Struggle for an Existence." Ah ha, I thought. At last! But what did I get? Something called the mistiltoe which needs the apple tree and there's too many seeds and all are going to die except one . . . ! No, Hally.

HALLY (*Intellectually outraged*) What do you mean, No! The poor man had to start somewhere. For God's sake, Sam, he revolutionized science. Now we know.

SAM What?

HALLY Where we come from and what it all means.

SAM And that's a benefit to mankind? Anyway, I still don't believe it.

HALLY God, you're impossible. I showed it to you in black and white.

SAM Doesn't mean I got to believe it.

HALLY It's the likes of you that kept the Inquisition in business. It's called bigotry. Anyway, that's my man of magnitude. Charles Darwin! Who's yours?

SAM (*Without hesitation*) Abraham Lincoln.

HALLY I might have guessed as much. Don't get sentimental, Sam. You've never been a slave, you know. And anyway we freed your ancestors here in South Africa long before the Americans. But if you want to thank somebody on their behalf, do it to Mr. William Wilberforce. Come on. Try again. I want a real genius. (*Now enjoying himself, and so is* SAM. HALLY *goes behind the counter and helps himself to a chocolate*)

SAM William Shakespeare.

HALLY (*No enthusiasm*) Oh. So you're also one of them, are you? You're basing that opinion on only one play, you know. You've only read my *Julius Caesar* and even I don't understand half of what they're talking about. They should do what they did with the old Bible: bring the language up to date.

SAM That's all you've got. It's also the only one *you've* read.

HALLY I know. I admit it. That's why I suggest we reserve our judgment until we've checked up on a few others. I've got a feeling, though, that by the end of this year one is going to be enough for me, and I can give you the names of twenty-nine other chaps in the Standard Nine class of the Port Elizabeth Technical College who feel the same. But if you want him, you can have him. My turn now. (*Pacing*) This is a

damned good exercise, you know! It started off looking like a simple question and here it's got us really probing into the intellectual heritage of our civilization.

SAM So who is it going to be?

HALLY My next man . . . and he gets the title on two scores: social reform and literary genius . . . is Leo Nikolaevich Tolstoy.

SAM That Russian.

HALLY Correct. Remember the picture of him I showed you?

SAM With the long beard.

HALLY (*Trying to look like Tolstoy*) And those burning, visionary eyes. My God, the face of a social prophet if ever I saw one! And remember my words when I showed it to you? Here's a *man*, Sam!

SAM Those were words, Hally.

HALLY Not many intellectuals are prepared to shovel manure with the peasants and then go home and write a "little book" called *War and Peace*. Incidentally, Sam, he was somebody else who, to quote, ". . . did not distinguish himself scholastically."

SAM Meaning?

HALLY He was also no good at school.

SAM Like you and Winston Churchill.

HALLY (*Mirthlessly*) Ha, ha, ha.

SAM (*Simultaneously*) Ha, ha, ha.

HALLY Don't get clever, Sam. That man freed his serfs of his own free will.

SAM No argument. He was a somebody, all right. I accept him.

HALLY I'm sure Count Tolstoy will be very pleased to

hear that. Your turn. Shoot. (*Another chocolate from behind the counter*) I'm waiting, Sam.

SAM I've got him.

HALLY Good. Submit your candidate for examination.

SAM Jesus.

HALLY (*Stopped dead in his tracks*) Who?

SAM Jesus Christ.

HALLY Oh, come on, Sam!

SAM The Messiah.

HALLY Ja, but still . . . No, Sam. Don't let's get started on religion. We'll just spend the whole afternoon arguing again. Suppose I turn around and say Mohammed?

SAM All right.

HALLY You can't have them both on the same list!

SAM Why not? You like Mohammed, I like Jesus.

HALLY I *don't* like Mohammed. I never have. I was merely being hypothetical. As far as I'm concerned, the Koran is as bad as the Bible. No. Religion is out! I'm not going to waste my time again arguing with you about the existence of God. You know perfectly well I'm an atheist . . . and I've got homework to do.

SAM Okay, I take him back.

HALLY You've got time for one more name.

SAM (*After thought*) I've got one I know we'll agree on. A simple straightforward great Man of Magnitude . . . and no arguments. And *he* really *did* benefit all mankind.

HALLY I wonder. After your last contribution I'm beginning to doubt whether anything in the way of an intellectual agreement is possible between the two of us. Who is he?

SAM Guess.

HALLY Socrates? Alexandre Dumas? Karl Marx? Dostoevsky? Nietzsche?

(SAM *shakes his head after each name*)

Give me a clue.

SAM The letter P is important . . .

HALLY Plato!

SAM . . . and his name begins with an F.

HALLY I've got it. Freud and Psychology.

SAM No. I didn't understand him.

HALLY That makes two of us.

SAM Think of mouldy apricot jam.

HALLY (*After a delighted laugh*) Penicillin and Sir Alexander Fleming! And the title of the book: *The Microbe Hunters.* (*Delighted*) Splendid, Sam! Splendid. For once we are in total agreement. The major breakthrough in medical science in the Twentieth Century. If it wasn't for him, we might have lost the Second World War. It's deeply gratifying, Sam, to know that I haven't been wasting my time in talking to you. (*Strutting around proudly*) Tolstoy may have educated his peasants, but I've educated you.

SAM Standard Four to Standard Nine.

HALLY Have we been at it as long as that?

SAM Yep. And my first lesson was geography.

HALLY (*Intrigued*) Really? I don't remember.

SAM My room there at the back of the old Jubilee Boarding House. I had just started working for your Mom. Little boy in short trousers walks in one afternoon and asks me seriously: "Sam, do you want to see South Africa?" Hey man! Sure I wanted to see South Africa!

HALLY Was that me?

SAM . . . So the next thing I'm looking at a map you had just done for homework. It was your first one and you were very proud of yourself.

HALLY Go on.

SAM Then came my first lesson. "Repeat after me, Sam: Gold in the Transvaal, mealies in the Free State, sugar in Natal and grapes in the Cape." I still know it!

HALLY Well, I'll be buggered. So that's how it all started.

SAM And your next map was one with all the rivers and the mountains they came from. The Orange, the Vaal, the Limpopo, the Zambezi . . .

HALLY You've got a phenomenal memory!

SAM You should be grateful. That is why you started passing your exams. You tried to be better than me.

(*They laugh together.* WILLIE *is attracted by the laughter and joins them*)

HALLY The old Jubilee Boarding House. Sixteen rooms with board and lodging, rent in advance and one week's notice. I haven't thought about it for donkey's years . . . and I don't think that's an accident. God, was I glad when we sold it and moved out. Those years are not remembered as the happiest ones of an unhappy childhood.

WILLIE (*Knocking on the table and trying to imitate a woman's voice*) "Hally, are you there?"

HALLY Who's that supposed to be?

WILLIE "What you doing in there, Hally? Come out at once!"

HALLY (*To* SAM) What's he talking about?

SAM Don't you remember?

WILLIE "Sam, Willie . . . is he in there with you boys?"

SAM Hiding away in our room when your mother was looking for you.

HALLY (*Another good laugh*) Of course! I used to crawl and hide under your bed! But finish the story, Willie. Then what used to happen? You chaps would give the game away by telling her I was in there with you. So much for friendship.

SAM We couldn't lie to her. She knew.

HALLY Which meant I got another rowing for hanging around the "servants' quarters." I think I spent more time in there with you chaps than anywhere else in that dump. And do you blame me? Nothing but bloody misery wherever you went. Somebody was always complaining about the food, or my mother was having a fight with Micky Nash because she'd caught her with a petty officer in her room. Maud Meiring was another one. Remember those two? They were prostitutes, you know. Soldiers and sailors from the troopships. Bottom fell out of the business when the war ended. God, the flotsam and jetsam that life washed up on our shores! No joking, if it wasn't for your room, I would have been the first certified ten-year-old in medical history. Ja, the memories are coming back now. Walking home from school and thinking: "What can I do this afternoon?" Try out a few ideas, but sooner or later I'd end up in there with you fellows. I bet you I could still find my way to your room with my eyes closed. (*He does exactly that*) Down the corridor . . . telephone on the right, which my Mom keeps locked because somebody is using it on the sly and not paying . . . past the kitchen and unappetizing cooking smells . . . around the corner into the backyard, hold my breath again because there are more smells coming when I pass your lavatory, then into that little passageway, first door on the right and into your room. How's that?

SAM Good. But, as usual, you forgot to knock.

HALLY Like that time I barged in and caught you and Cynthia . . . at it. Remember? God, was I embarrassed! I didn't know what was going on at first.

SAM Ja, that taught you a lesson.

HALLY And about a lot more than knocking on doors, I'll have you know, and I don't mean geography either. Hell, Sam, couldn't you have waited until it was dark?

SAM No.

HALLY Was it that urgent?

SAM Yes, and if you don't believe me, wait until your time comes.

HALLY No, thank you. I am not interested in girls. (*Back to his memories . . . Using a few chairs he recreates the room as he lists the items*) A gray little room with a cold cement floor. Your bed against that wall . . . and I now know why the mattress sags so much! . . . Willie's bed . . . it's propped up on bricks because one leg is broken . . . that wobbly little table with the washbasin and jug of water . . . Yes! . . . stuck to the wall above it are some pin-up pictures from magazines. Joe Louis . . .

WILLIE Brown Bomber. World Title. (*Boxing pose*) Three rounds and knockout.

HALLY Against who?

SAM Max Schmeling.

HALLY Correct. I can also remember Fred Astaire and Ginger Rogers, and Rita Hayworth in a bathing costume which always made me hot and bothered when I looked at it. Under Willie's bed is an old suitcase with all his clothes in a mess, which is why I never hide there. Your things are neat and tidy in a trunk next to your bed, and on it there is a picture of you and Cynthia in your ballroom clothes, your first silver cup for third place in a competition and an old radio which doesn't work anymore. Have I left out anything?

SAM No.

HALLY Right, so much for the stage directions. Now the characters. (SAM *and* WILLIE *move to their appropriate positions in the bedroom*) Willie is in bed, under his blankets with his clothes on, complaining nonstop about something, but we can't make out a word of what he's saying because he's got his head under the blankets as well. You're on your bed trimming your toenails with a knife—not a very edifying sight—and as for me . . . What am I doing?

SAM You're sitting on the floor giving Willie a lecture about being a good loser while you get the checker board and pieces ready for a game. Then you go to Willie's bed, pull off the blankets and make him play with you first because you know you're going to win, and that gives you the second game with me.

HALLY And you certainly were a bad loser, Willie!

WILLIE Haai!

HALLY Wasn't he, Sam? And so slow! A game with you almost took the whole afternoon. Thank God I gave up trying to teach you how to play chess.

WILLIE You and Sam cheated.

HALLY I never saw Sam cheat, and mine were mostly the mistakes of youth.

WILLIE Then how is it you two was always winning?

HALLY Have you ever considered the possibility, Willie, that it was because we were better than you?

WILLIE Every time better?

HALLY Not every time. There were occasions when we deliberately let you win a game so that you would stop sulking and go on playing with us. Sam used to wink at me when you weren't looking to show me it was time to let you win.

WILLIE So then you two didn't play fair.

HALLY It was for your benefit, Mr. Malopo, which is more than being fair. It was an act of self-sacrifice. (*To* SAM) But you know what my best memory is, don't you?

SAM No.

HALLY Come on, guess. If your memory is so good, you must remember it as well.

SAM We got up to a lot of tricks in there, Hally.

HALLY This one was special, Sam.

SAM I'm listening.

HALLY It started off looking like another of those useless nothing-to-do afternoons. I'd already been down to Main Street looking for adventure, but nothing had happened. I didn't feel like climbing trees in the Donkin Park or pretending I was a private eye and following a stranger . . . so as usual: See what's cooking in Sam's room. This time it was you on the floor. You had two thin pieces of wood and you were smoothing them down with a knife. It didn't look particularly interesting, but when I asked you what you were doing, you just said, "Wait and see, Hally. Wait . . . and see" . . . in that secret sort of way of yours, so I knew there was a surprise coming. You teased me, you bugger, by being deliberately slow and not answering my questions!

(SAM *laughs*)

And whistling while you worked away! God, it was infuriating! I could have brained you! It was only when you tied them together in a cross and put that down on the brown paper that I realized what you were doing. "Sam is making a kite?" And when I asked you and you said "Yes" . . . ! (*Shaking his head with disbelief*) The sheer audacity of it took my breath away. I mean, seriously, what the hell does a black man know about flying a kite? I'll be honest with you, Sam, I had no hopes for it. If you think I was excited and happy, you got another guess coming. In fact, I was shit-scared that we were going to make fools of ourselves. When we left the boarding house to go up onto the hill, I was praying quietly that there wouldn't be any other kids around to laugh at us.

SAM (*Enjoying the memory as much as* HALLY) Ja, I could see that.

HALLY I made it obvious, did I?

SAM Ja. You refused to carry it.

HALLY Do you blame me? Can you remember what the poor thing looked like? Tomato-box wood and brown paper! Flour and water for glue! Two of my mother's old stockings for a tail, and then all those bits and pieces of string you made me tie together so that we could fly it! Hell, no, that was now only asking for a miracle to happen.

SAM Then the big argument when I told you to hold the string and run with it when I let go.

HALLY I was prepared to run, all right, but straight back to the boarding house.

SAM (*Knowing what's coming*) So what happened?

HALLY Come on, Sam, you remember as well as I do.

SAM I want to hear it from you.

(HALLY *pauses. He wants to be as accurate as possible*)

HALLY You went a little distance from me down the hill, you held it up ready to let it go. . . . "This is it," I thought. "Like everything else in my life, here comes another fiasco." Then you shouted, "Go, Hally!" and

I started to run. (*Another pause*) I don't know how to describe it, Sam. Ja! The miracle happened! I was running, waiting for it to crash to the ground, but instead suddenly there was something alive behind me at the end of the string, tugging at it as if it wanted to be free. I looked back . . . (*Shakes his head*) . . . I still can't believe my eyes. It was flying! Looping around and trying to climb even higher into the sky. You shouted to me to let it have more string. I did, until there was none left and I was just holding that piece of wood we had tied it to. You came up and joined me. You were laughing.

SAM So were you. And shouting, "It works, Sam! We've done it!"

HALLY And we had! I was so proud of us! It was the most splendid thing I had ever seen. I wished there were hundreds of kids around to watch us. The part that scared me, though, was when you showed me how to make it dive down to the ground and then just when it was on the point of crashing, swoop up again!

SAM You didn't want to try yourself.

HALLY Of course not! I would have been suicidal if anything had happened to it. Watching you do it made me nervous enough. I was quite happy just to see it up there with its tail fluttering behind it. You left me after that, didn't you? You explained how to get it down, we tied it to the bench so that I could sit and watch it, and you went away. I wanted you to stay, you know. I was a little scared of having to look after it by myself.

SAM (*Quietly*) I had work to do, Hally.

HALLY It was sort of sad bringing it down, Sam. And it looked sad again when it was lying there on the ground. Like something that had lost its soul. Just tomato-box wood, brown paper and two of my mother's old stockings! But, hell, I'll never forget that first moment when I saw it up there. I had a stiff neck the next day from looking up so much.

(SAM *laughs.* HALLY *turns to him with a question he never thought of asking before*)

Why did you make that kite, Sam?

SAM (*Evenly*) I can't remember.

HALLY Truly?

SAM Too long ago, Hally.

HALLY Ja, I suppose it was. It's time for another one, you know.

SAM Why do you say that?

HALLY Because it feels like that. Wouldn't be a good day to fly it, though.

SAM No. You can't fly kites on rainy days.

HALLY (*He studies* SAM. *Their memories have made him conscious of the man's presence in his life*) How old are you, Sam?

SAM Two score and five.

HALLY Strange, isn't it?

SAM What?

HALLY Me and you.

SAM What's strange about it?

HALLY Little white boy in short trousers and a black man old enough to be his father flying a kite. It's not every day you see that.

SAM But why strange? Because the one is white and the other black?

HALLY I don't know. Would have been just as strange, I suppose, if it had been me and my Dad . . . cripple man and a little boy! Nope! There's no chance of me flying a kite without it being strange. (*Simple state-*

ment of fact—no self-pity) There's a nice little short story there. "The Kite-Flyers." But we'd have to find a twist in the ending.

SAM Twist?

HALLY Yes. Something unexpected. The way it ended with us was too straightforward . . . me on the bench and you going back to work. There's no drama in that.

WILLIE And me?

HALLY You?

WILLIE Yes me.

HALLY You want to get into the story as well, do you? I got it! Change the title: "Afternoons in Sam's Room" . . . expand it and tell all the stories. It's on its way to being a novel. Our days in the old Jubilee. Sad in a way that they're over. I almost wish we were still in that little room.

SAM We're still together.

HALLY That's true. It's just that life felt the right size in there . . . not too big and not too small. Wasn't so hard to work up a bit of courage. It's got so bloody complicated since then.

(*The telephone rings.* SAM *answers it*)

SAM St. George's Park Tea Room . . . Hello, Madam . . . Yes, Madam, he's here. . . . Hally, it's your mother.

HALLY Where is she phoning from?

SAM Sounds like the hospital. It's a public telephone.

HALLY (*Relieved*) You see! I told you. (*The telephone*) Hello, Mom . . . Yes . . . Yes no fine. Everything's under control here. How's things with poor old Dad? . . . Has he had a bad turn? . . . What? . . . Oh, God! . . . Yes, Sam told me, but I was sure he'd made a mistake. But what's this all about, Mom? He didn't look at all good last night. How can he get better so quickly? . . . Then very obviously you must say no. Be firm with him. You're the boss. . . . You know what it's going to be like if he comes home. . . . Well then, don't blame me when I fail my exams at the end of the year. . . . Yes! How am I expected to be fresh for school when I spend half the night massaging his gammy leg? . . . So am I! . . . So tell him a white lie. Say Dr. Colley wants more X-rays of his stump. Or bribe him. We'll sneak in double tots of brandy in future. . . . What? . . . Order him to get back into bed at once! If he's going to behave like a child, treat him like one. . . . All right, Mom! I was just trying to . . . I'm sorry. . . . I said I'm sorry. . . . Quick, give me your number. I'll phone you back. (*He hangs up and waits a few seconds*) Here we go again! (*He dials*) I'm sorry, Mom. . . . Okay . . . But now listen to me carefully. All it needs is for you to put your foot down. Don't take no for an answer. . . . Did you hear me? And whatever you do, don't discuss it with him. . . . Because I'm frightened you'll give in to him. . . . Yes, Sam gave me lunch. . . . I ate all of it! . . . No, Mom not a soul. It's still raining here. . . . Right, I'll tell them. I'll just do some homework and then lock up. . . . But remember now, Mom. Don't listen to anything he says. And phone me back and let me know what happens. . . . Okay. Bye, Mom. (*He hangs up. The men are staring at him*) My Mom says that when you're finished with the floors you must do the windows. (*Pause*) Don't misunderstand me, chaps. All I want is for him to get better. And if he was, I'd be the first person to say: "Bring him home." But he's not, and we can't give him the medical care and attention he needs at home. That's what hospitals are there for. (*Brusquely*) So don't just stand there! Get on with it!

(SAM *clears* HALLY'S *table*)

You heard right. My Dad wants to go home.

SAM Is he better?

HALLY (*Sharply*) No! How the hell can he be better when last night he was groaning with pain? This is not an age of miracles!

SAM Then he should stay in hospital.

HALLY (*Seething with irritation and frustration*) Tell me something I don't know, Sam. What the hell do you think I was saying to my Mom? All I can say is fuck-it-all.

SAM I'm sure he'll listen to your Mom.

HALLY You don't know what she's up against. He's already packed his shaving kit and pajamas and is sitting on his bed with his crutches, dressed and ready to go. I know him when he gets in that mood. If she tries to reason with him, we've had it. She's no match for him when it comes to a battle of words. He'll tie her up in knots. (*Trying to hide his true feelings*)

SAM I suppose it gets lonely for him in there.

HALLY With all the patients and nurses around? Regular visits from the Salvation Army? Balls! It's ten times worse for him at home. I'm at school and my mother is here in the business all day.

SAM He's at least got you at night.

HALLY (*Before he can stop himself*) And we've got him! Please! I don't want to talk about it anymore. (*Unpacks his school case, slamming down books on the table*) Life is just a plain bloody mess, that's all. And people are fools.

SAM Come on, Hally.

HALLY Yes, they are! They bloody well deserve what they get.

SAM Then don't complain.

HALLY Don't try to be clever, Sam. It doesn't suit you. Anybody who thinks there's nothing wrong with this world needs to have his head examined. Just when things are going along all right, without fail someone or something will come along and spoil everything. Somebody should write that down as a fundamental law of the Universe. The principle of perpetual disappointment. If there is a God who created this world, he should scrap it and try again.

SAM All right, Hally, all right. What you got for homework?

HALLY Bullshit, as usual. (*Opens an exercise book and reads*) "Write five hundred words describing an annual event of cultural or historical significance."

SAM That should be easy enough for you.

HALLY And also plain bloody boring. You know what he wants, don't you? One of their useless old ceremonies. The commemoration of the landing of the 1820 Settlers, or if it's going to be culture, Carols by Candlelight every Christmas.

SAM It's an impressive sight. Make a good description, Hally. All those candles glowing in the dark and the people singing hymns.

HALLY And it's called religious hysteria. (*Intense irritation*) Please, Sam! Just leave me alone and let me get on with it. I'm not in the mood for games this afternoon. And remember my Mom's orders . . . you're to help Willie with the windows. Come on now, I don't want any more nonsense in here.

SAM Okay, Hally, okay.

(HALLY *settles down to his homework; determined preparations . . . pen, ruler, exercise book, dictionary, another cake . . . all of which will lead to nothing*)

(SAM *waltzes over to* WILLIE *and starts to replace tables and chairs. He practices a ballroom step while doing so.* WILLIE *watches. When* SAM *is finished,* WILLIE *tries*) Good! But just a little bit quicker on the turn and only move in to her after she's crossed over. What about this one?

(*Another step. When* SAM *is finished,* WILLIE *again has a go*)

Much better. See what happens when you just relax and enjoy yourself? Remember that in two weeks' time and you'll be all right.

WILLIE But I haven't got partner, Boet Sam.

SAM Maybe Hilda will turn up tonight.

WILLIE No, Boet Sam. (*Reluctantly*) I gave her a good hiding.

SAM You mean a bad one.

WILLIE Good bad one.

SAM Then you mustn't complain either. Now you pay the price for losing your temper.

WILLIE I also pay two pounds ten shilling entrance fee.

SAM They'll refund you if you withdraw now.

WILLIE (*Appalled*) You mean, don't dance?

SAM Yes.

WILLIE No! I wait too long and I practice too hard. If I find me new partner, you think I can be ready in two weeks? I ask Madam for my leave now and we practice every day.

SAM Quickstep non-stop for two weeks. World record, Willie, but you'll be mad at the end.

WILLIE No jokes, Boet Sam.

SAM I'm not joking.

WILLIE So then what?

SAM Find Hilda. Say you're sorry and promise you won't beat her again.

WILLIE No.

SAM Then withdraw. Try again next year.

WILLIE No.

SAM Then I give up.

WILLIE Haaikona, Boet Sam, you can't.

SAM What do you mean, I can't? I'm telling you: I give up.

WILLIE (*Adamant*) No! (*Accusingly*) It was you who start me ballroom dancing.

SAM So?

WILLIE Before that I use to be happy. And is you and Miriam who bring me to Hilda and say here's partner for you.

SAM What are you saying, Willie?

WILLIE You!

SAM But me what? To blame?

WILLIE Yes.

SAM Willie . . . ? (*Bursts into laughter*)

WILLIE And now all you do is make jokes at me. You wait. When Miriam leaves you is my turn to laugh. Ha! Ha! Ha!

SAM (*He can't take* WILLIE *seriously any longer*) She can leave me tonight! I know what to do. (*Bowing before an imaginary partner*) May I have the pleasure? (*He dances and sings*)
"Just a fellow with his pillow . . .
Dancin' like a willow . . .
In an autumn breeze . . ."

WILLIE There you go again!

(SAM *goes on dancing and singing*)

Boet Sam!

SAM There's the answer to your problem! Judges' announcement in two weeks' time: "Ladies and gentlemen, the winner in the open section . . . Mr. Willie Malopo and his pillow!"

(*This is too much for a now really angry* WILLIE. *He goes for* SAM, *but the latter is too quick for him and puts* HALLY'S *table between the two of them*)

HALLY (*Exploding*) For Christ's sake, you two!

WILLIE (*Still trying to get at* SAM) I donner you, Sam! Struesgod!

SAM (*Still laughing*) Sorry, Willie . . . Sorry . . .

HALLY Sam! Willie! (*Grabs his ruler and gives* WILLIE *a vicious whack on the bum*) How the hell am I supposed to concentrate with the two of you behaving like bloody children!

WILLIE Hit him too!

HALLY Shut up, Willie.

WILLIE He started jokes again.

HALLY Get back to your work. You too, Sam. (*His ruler*) Do you want another one, Willie?

(SAM *and* WILLIE *return to their work.* HALLY *uses the opportunity to escape from his unsuccessful attempt at homework. He struts around like a little despot, ruler in hand, giving vent to his anger and frustration*)

Suppose a customer had walked in then? Or the Park Superintendent. And seen the two of you behaving like a pair of hooligans. That would have been the end of my mother's license, you know. And your jobs! Well, this is the end of it. From now on there will be no more of your ballroom nonsense in here. This is a business establishment, not a bloody New Brighton dancing school. I've been far too lenient with the two of you. (*Behind the counter for a green cool drink and a dollop of ice cream. He keeps up his tirade as he prepares it*) But what really makes me bitter is that I allow you chaps a little freedom in here when business is bad and what do you do with it? The foxtrot! Specially you, Sam. There's more to life than trotting around a dance floor and I thought at least you knew it.

SAM It's a harmless pleasure, Hally. It doesn't hurt anybody.

HALLY It's also a rather simple one, you know.

SAM You reckon so? Have you ever tried?

HALLY Of course not.

SAM Why don't you? Now.

HALLY What do you mean? Me dance?

SAM Yes. I'll show you a simple step—the waltz—then you try it.

HALLY What will that prove?

SAM That it might not be as easy as you think.

HALLY I didn't say it was easy. I said it was simple—like in simple-minded, meaning mentally retarded. You can't exactly say it challenges the intellect.

SAM It does other things.

HALLY Such as?

SAM Make people happy.

HALLY (*The glass in his hand*) So do American cream sodas with ice cream. For God's sake, Sam, you're not asking me to take ballroom dancing serious, are you?

SAM Yes.

HALLY (*Sigh of defeat*) Oh, well, so much for trying to give you a decent education. I've obviously achieved nothing.

SAM You still haven't told me what's wrong with admiring something that's beautiful and then trying to do it yourself.

HALLY Nothing. But we happen to be talking about a foxtrot, not a thing of beauty.

SAM But that is just what I'm saying. If you were to see two champions doing, two masters of the art . . . !

HALLY Oh, God, I give up. So now it's also art!

SAM Ja.

HALLY There's a limit, Sam. Don't confuse art and entertainment.

SAM So then what is art?

HALLY You want a definition?

SAM Ja.

HALLY (*He realizes he has got to be careful. He gives the matter a lot of thought before answering*) Philosophers have been trying to do that for centuries. What is Art? What is Life? But basically I suppose it's . . . the giving of meaning to matter.

SAM Nothing to do with beautiful?

HALLY It goes beyond that. It's the giving of form to the formless.

SAM Ja, well, maybe it's not art, then. But I still say it's beautiful.

HALLY I'm sure the word you mean to use is entertaining.

SAM (*Adamant*) No. Beautiful. And if you want proof, come along to the Centenary Hall in New Brighton in two weeks' time.

(*The mention of the Centenary Hall draws* WILLIE *over to them*)

HALLY What for? I've seen the two of you prancing around in here often enough.

SAM (*He laughs*) This isn't the real thing, Hally. We're just playing around in here.

HALLY So? I can use my imagination.

SAM And what do you get?

HALLY A lot of people dancing around and having a so-called good time.

SAM That all?

HALLY Well, basically it is that, surely.

SAM No, it isn't. Your imagination hasn't helped you at all. There's a lot more to it than that. We're getting ready for the championships, Hally, not just another dance. There's going to be a lot of people, all right, and they're going to have a good time, but they'll only be spectators, sitting around and watching. It's just the competitors out there on the dance floor. Party decorations and fancy lights all around the walls! The ladies in beautiful evening dresses!

HALLY My mother's got one of those, Sam, and, quite frankly, it's an embarrassment every time she wears it.

SAM (*Undeterred*) Your imagination left out the excitement.

(HALLY *scoffs*)

Oh, yes. The finalists are not going to be out there just to have a good time. One of those couples will be the 1950 Eastern Province Champions. And your imagination left out the music.

WILLIE Mr. Elijah Gladman Guzana and his Orchestral Jazzonions.

SAM The sound of the big band, Hally. Trombone, trumpet, tenor and alto sax. And then, finally, your imagination also left out the climax of the evening when the dancing is finished, the judges have stopped whispering among themselves and the Master of Ceremonies collects their scorecards and goes up onto the stage to announce the winners.

HALLY All right. So you make it sound like a bit of a do. It's an occasion. Satisfied?

SAM (*Victory*) So you admit that!

HALLY Emotionally yes, intellectually no.

SAM Well, I don't know what you mean by that, all I'm telling you is that it is going to be *the* event of the year in New Brighton. It's been sold out for two weeks already. There's only standing room left. We've got competitors coming from Kingwilliamstown, East London, Port Alfred.

(HALLY *starts pacing thoughtfully*)

HALLY Tell me a bit more.

SAM I thought you weren't interested . . . intellectually.

HALLY (*Mysteriously*) I've got my reasons.

SAM What do you want to know?

HALLY It takes place every year?

SAM Yes. But only every third year in New Brighton. It's East London's turn to have the championships next year.

HALLY Which, I suppose, makes it an even more significant event.

SAM Ah ha! We're getting somewhere. Our "occasion" is now a "significant event."

HALLY I wonder.

SAM What?

HALLY I wonder if I would get away with it.

SAM But what?

HALLY (*To the table and his exercise book*) "Write five hundred words describing an annual event of cultural or historical significance." Would I be stretching poetic license a little too far if I called your ballroom championships a cultural event?

SAM You mean . . . ?

HALLY You think we could get five hundred words out of it, Sam?

SAM Victor Sylvester has written a whole book on ballroom dancing.

WILLIE You going to write about it, Master Hally?

HALLY Yes, gentlemen, that is precisely what I am considering doing. Old Doc Bromely—he's my English teacher—is going to argue with me, of course. He doesn't like natives. But I'll point out to him that in strict anthropological terms the culture of a primitive black society includes its dancing and singing. To put my thesis in a nutshell: The war-dance has been replaced by the waltz. But it still amounts to the same thing: the release of primitive emotions through movement. Shall we give it a go?

SAM I'm ready.

WILLIE Me also.

HALLY Ha! This will teach the old bugger a lesson. (*Decision taken*) Right. Let's get ourselves organized. (*This means another cake on the table. He sits*) I think you've given me enough general atmosphere, Sam, but to build the tension and suspense I need facts. (*Pencil poised*)

WILLIE Give him facts, Boet Sam.

HALLY What you called the climax . . . how many finalists?

SAM Six couples.

HALLY (*Making notes*) Go on. Give me the picture.

SAM Spectators seated right around the hall. (WILLIE *becomes a spectator*)

HALLY . . . and it's a full house.

SAM At one end, on the stage, Gladman and his Orchestral Jazzonions. At the other end is a long table with the three judges. The six finalists go onto the dance floor and take up their positions. When they are ready and the spectators have settled down, the Master of Ceremonies goes to the microphone. To start with, he makes some jokes to get the people laughing . . .

HALLY Good touch! (*As he writes*) ". . . creating a relaxed atmosphere which will change to one of tension and drama as the climax is approached."

SAM (*Onto a chair to act out the M.C.*) "Ladies and gentlemen, we come now to the great moment you have all been waiting for this evening. . . . The finals of the 1950 Eastern Province Open Ballroom Dancing Championships. But first let me introduce the finalists! Mr. and Mrs. Welcome Tchabalala from Kingwilliamstown . . ."

WILLIE (*He applauds after every name*) Is when the people clap their hands and whistle and make a lot of noise, Master Hally.

SAM "Mr. Mulligan Njikelane and Miss Nomhle Nkonyeni of Grahamstown; Mr. and Mrs. Norman Nchinga from Port Alfred; Mr. Fats Bokolane and Miss Dina Plaatjies from East London; Mr. Sipho Dugu and Mrs. Mable Magada from Peddie; and from New Brighton our very own Mr. Willie Malopo and Miss Hilda Samuels."

(WILLIE *can't believe his ears. He abandons his role as spectator and scrambles into position as a finalist*)

WILLIE Relaxed and ready to romance!

SAM The applause dies down. When everybody is silent, Gladman lifts up his sax, nods at the Orchestral Jazzonions . . .

WILLIE Play the jukebox please, Boet Sam!

SAM I also only got bus fare, Willie.

HALLY Hold it, everybody. (*Heads for the cash register behind the counter*) How much is in the till, Sam?

SAM Three shillings. Hally . . . your Mom counted it before she left.

(HALLY *hesitates*)

HALLY Sorry, Willie. You know how she carried on the last time I did it. We'll just have to pool our combined imaginations and hope for the best. (*Returns to the table*) Back to work. How are the points scored, Sam?

SAM Maximum of ten points each for individual style, deportment, rhythm and general appearance.

WILLIE Must I start?

HALLY Hold it for a second, Willie. And penalties?

SAM For what?

HALLY For doing something wrong. Say you stumble or bump into somebody . . . do they take off any points?

SAM (*Aghast*) Hally . . . !

HALLY When you're dancing. If you and your partner collide into another couple.

(HALLY *can get no further.* SAM *has collapsed with laughter. He explains to* WILLIE)

SAM If me and Miriam bump into you and Hilda . . .

(WILLIE *joins him in another good laugh*)

Hally, Hally . . . !

HALLY (*Perplexed*) Why? What did I say?

SAM There's no collisions out there, Hally. Nobody trips or stumbles or bumps into anybody else. That's what that moment is all about. To be one of those finalists on that dance floor is like . . . like being in a dream about a world in which accidents don't happen.

HALLY (*Genuinely moved by* SAM'S *image*) Jesus, Sam! That's beautiful!

WILLIE (*Can endure waiting no longer*) I'm starting! (WILLIE *dances while* SAM *talks*)

SAM Of course it is. That's what I've been trying to say to you all afternoon. And it's beautiful because that is what we want life to be like. But instead, like you said, Hally, we're bumping into each other all the time. Look at the three of us this afternoon: I've bumped into Willie, the two of us have bumped into you, you've bumped into your mother, she bumping into your Dad. . . . None of us knows the steps and there's no music playing. And it doesn't stop with us. The whole world is doing it all the time. Open a newspaper and what do you read? America has bumped into Russia, England is bumping into India, rich man bumps into poor man. Those are big collisions, Hally. They make for a lot of bruises. People get hurt in all that bumping, and we're sick and tired of it now. It's been going on for too long. Are we never going to get it right? . . . Learn to dance life like champions instead of always being just a bunch of beginners at it?

HALLY (*Deep and sincere admiration of the man*) You've got a vision, Sam!

SAM Not just me. What I'm saying to you is that everybody's got it. That's why there's only standing room left for the Centenary Hall in two weeks' time. For as long as the music lasts, we are going to see six couples get it right, the way we want life to be.

HALLY But is that the best we can do, Sam . . . watch six finalists dreaming about the way it should be?

SAM I don't know. But it starts with that. Without the dream we won't know what we're going for. And anyway I reckon there are a few people who have got past just dreaming about it and are trying for something real. Remember that thing we read once in the paper about the Mahatma Gandhi? Going without food to stop those riots in India?

HALLY You're right. He certainly was trying to teach people to get the steps right.

SAM And the Pope.

HALLY Yes, he's another one. Our old General Smuts as well, you know. He's also out there dancing. You know, Sam, when you come to think of it, that's what the United Nations boils down to . . . a dancing school for politicians!

SAM And let's hope they learn.

HALLY (*A little surge of hope*) You're right. We mustn't despair. Maybe there's some hope for mankind after all. Keep it up, Willie. (*Back to his table with determination*) This is a lot bigger than I thought. So what have we got? Yes, our title: "A World Without Collisions."

SAM That sounds good! "A World Without Collisions."

HALLY Subtitle: "Global Politics on the Dance Floor." No. A bit too heavy, hey? What about "Ballroom Dancing as a Political Vision"?

(*The telephone rings.* SAM *answers it*)

SAM St. George's Park Tea Room . . . Yes, Madam . . . Hally, it's your Mom.

HALLY (*Back to reality*) Oh, God, yes! I'd forgotten all about that. Shit! Remember my words, Sam? Just when you're enjoying yourself, someone or something will come along and wreck everything.

SAM You haven't heard what she's got to say yet.

HALLY Public telephone?

SAM No.

HALLY Does she sound happy or unhappy?

SAM I couldn't tell. (*Pause*) She's waiting, Hally.

HALLY (*To the telephone*) Hello, Mom . . . No, everything is okay here. Just doing my homework. . . . What's your news? . . . You've what? . . . (*Pause. He takes the receiver away from his ear for a few seconds. In the course of* HALLY'S *telephone conversation,* SAM *and* WILLIE *discretely position the stacked tables and chairs.* HALLY *places the receiver back to his ear*) Yes, I'm still here. Oh, well, I give up now. Why did you do it, Mom? . . . Well, I just hope you know what you've let us in for. . . . (*Loudly*) I said I hope you know what you've let us in for! It's the end of the peace and quiet we've been having. (*Softly*) Where is he? (*Normal voice*) He can't hear us from in there. But for God's sake, Mom, what happened? I told you to be firm with him. . . . Then you and the nurses should have held him down, taken his crutches away. . . . I know only too well he's my father! . . . I'm not being disrespectful, but I'm sick and tired of emptying stinking chamberpots full of phlegm and piss. . . . Yes, I do! When you're not there, he asks *me* to do it. . . . If you really want to know the truth, that's why I've got no appetite for my food. . . . Yes! There's a lot of things you don't know about. For your information, I still haven't got that science textbook I need. And you know why? He borrowed the money you gave me for it. . . . Because I didn't want to start another fight between you two. . . . He says that every time. . . . All right, Mom! (*Viciously*) Then just remember to start hiding your bag away again, because he'll be at your purse before long for money for booze. And when he's well enough to come down here, you better keep an eye on the till as well, because that is also going to develop a leak. . . . Then don't complain to me when he starts his old tricks. . . . Yes, you do. I get it from you on one side and from him on the other, and it makes life hell for me. I'm not going to be the peacemaker anymore. I'm warning you now: when the two of you start fighting again, I'm leaving home. . . . Mom, if you start crying, I'm going to put down the receiver. . . . Okay . . . (*Lowering his voice to a vicious whisper*) Okay, Mom. I heard you. (*Desperate*) No. . . . Because I don't want to. I'll see him when I get home! Mom! . . . (*Pause. When he speaks again, his tone changes completely. It is not simply pretense. We sense a genuine emotional conflict*) Welcome home, chum! . . . What's that? . . . Don't be silly, Dad. You being home is just about the best news in the world. . . . I bet you are. Bloody depressing there with everybody going on about their ailments, hey! . . . How you feeling? . . . Good . . . Here as well, pal. Coming down cats and dogs. . . . That's right. Just the day for a kip and a toss in your old Uncle Ned. . . . Everything's just hunky-dory on my side, Dad. . . . Well, to start with, there's a nice pile of comics for you on the counter. . . . Yes, old Kemple brought them in. *Batman and Robin, Submariner* . . . just your cup of tea . . . I will. . . . Yes, we'll spin a few yarns tonight. . . . Okay, chum, see you in a little while. . . . No, I promise. I'll come straight home. . . . (*Pause—his mother comes back on the phone*) Mom? Okay. I'll lock up now. . . . What? . . . Oh, the brandy . . . Yes, I'll remember! . . . I'll put it in my suitcase now, for God's sake. I know well enough what will happen if he doesn't get it. . . . (*Places a bottle of brandy on the counter*) I *was* kind to him, Mom. I didn't say anything nasty! . . . All right. Bye. (*End of telephone conversation. A desolate* HALLY *doesn't move. A strained silence*)

SAM (*Quietly*) That sounded like a bad bump, Hally.

HALLY (*Having a hard time controlling his emotions. He speaks carefully*) Mind your own business, Sam.

SAM Sorry. I wasn't trying to interfere. Shall we carry

on? Hally? (*He indicates the exercise book. No response from* HALLY)

WILLIE (*Also trying*) Tell him about when they give out the cups, Boet Sam.

SAM Ja! That's another big moment. The presentation of the cups after the winners have been announced. You've got to put that in.

(*Still no response from* HALLY)

WILLIE A big silver one, Master Hally, called floating trophy for the champions.

SAM We always invite some big-shot personality to hand them over. Guest of honor this year is going to be His Holiness Bishop Jabulani of the All African Free Zionist Church.

(HALLY *gets up abruptly, goes to his table and tears up the page he was writing on*)

HALLY So much for a bloody world without collisions.

SAM Too bad. It was on its way to being a good composition.

HALLY Let's stop bullshitting ourselves, Sam.

SAM Have we been doing that?

HALLY Yes! That's what all our talk about a decent world has been . . . just so much bullshit.

SAM We did say it was still only a dream.

HALLY And a bloody useless one at that. Life's a fuck-up and it's never going to change.

SAM Ja, maybe that's true.

HALLY There's no maybe about it. It's a blunt and brutal fact. All we've done this afternoon is waste our time.

SAM Not if we'd got your homework done.

HALLY I don't give a shit about my homework, so, for Christ's sake, just shut up about it. (*Slamming books viciously into his school case*) Hurry up now and finish your work. I want to lock up and get out of here. (*Pause*) And then go where? Home-sweet-fucking-home. Jesus, I hate that word.

(HALLY *goes to the counter to put the brandy bottle and comics in his school case. After a moment's hesitation, he smashes the bottle of brandy. He abandons all further attempts to hide his feelings.* SAM *and* WILLIE *work away as unobtrusively as possible*)

Do you want to know what is really wrong with your lovely little dream, Sam? It's not just that we are all bad dancers. That does happen to be perfectly true, but there's more to it than just that. You left out the cripples.

SAM Hally!

HALLY (*Now totally reckless*) Ja! Can't leave them out, Sam. That's why we always end up on our backsides on the dance floor. They're also out there dancing . . . like a bunch of broken spiders trying to do the quick-step! (*An ugly attempt at laughter*) When you come to think of it, it's a bloody comical sight. I mean, it's bad enough on two legs . . . but one and a pair of crutches! Hell, no, Sam. That's guaranteed to turn that dance floor into a shambles. Why you shaking your head? Picture it, man. For once this afternoon let's use our imaginations sensibly.

SAM Be careful, Hally.

HALLY Of what? The truth? I seem to be the only one around here who is prepared to face it. We've had the pretty dream, it's time now to wake up and have a good long look at the way things really are. Nobody knows the steps, there's no music, the cripples are also out there tripping up everybody and trying to get into the act, and it's all called the All-Comers-How-to-Make-a-Fuckup-of-Life Championships. (*Another ugly laugh*) Hang on, Sam! The best bit is still coming. Do you know what the winner's trophy is? A beautiful big chamber-pot with roses on the side, and it's full to the brim with piss. And guess who I think is going to be this year's winner.

SAM (*Almost shouting*) Stop now!

HALLY (*Suddenly appalled by how far he has gone*) Why?

SAM Hally? It's your father you're talking about.

HALLY So?

SAM Do you know what you've been saying?

(HALLY *can't answer. He is rigid with shame.* SAM *speaks to him sternly*)

No, Hally, you mustn't do it. Take back those words and ask for forgiveness! It's a terrible sin for a son to mock his father with jokes like that. You'll be punished if you carry on. Your father is your father, even if he is a . . . cripple man.

WILLIE Yes, Master Hally. Is true what Sam say.

SAM I understand how you are feeling, Hally, but even so . . .

HALLY No, you don't!

SAM I think I do.

HALLY And I'm telling you you don't. Nobody does. (*Speaking carefully as his shame turns to rage at* SAM) It's your turn to be careful, Sam. Very careful! You're treading on dangerous ground. Leave me and my father alone.

SAM I'm not the one who's been saying things about him.

HALLY What goes on between me and my Dad is none of your business!

SAM Then don't tell me about it. If that's all you've got to say about him, I don't want to hear.

(*For a moment* HALLY *is at loss for a response*)

HALLY Just get on with your bloody work and shut up.

SAM Swearing at me won't help you.

HALLY Yes, it does! Mind your own fucking business and shut up!

SAM Okay. If that's the way you want it, I'll stop trying.

(*He turns away. This infuriates* HALLY *even more*)

HALLY Good. Because what you've been trying to do is meddle in something you know nothing about. All that concerns you in here, Sam, is to try and do what you get paid for—keep the place clean and serve the customers. In plain words, just get on with your job. My mother is right. She's always warning me about allowing you to get too familiar. Well, this time you've gone too far. It's going to stop right now.

(*No response from* SAM)

You're only a servant in here, and don't forget it.

(*Still no response.* HALLY *is trying hard to get one*)

And as far as my father is concerned, all you need to remember is that he is your boss.

SAM (*Needled at last*) No, he isn't. I get paid by your mother.

HALLY Don't argue with me, Sam!

SAM Then don't say he's my boss.

HALLY He's a white man and that's good enough for you.

SAM I'll try to forget you said that.

HALLY Don't! Because you won't be doing me a favor if you do. I'm telling you to remember it.

(*A pause.* SAM *pulls himself together and makes one last effort*)

SAM Hally, Hally . . . ! Come on now. Let's stop before it's too late. You're right. We *are* on dangerous ground. If we're not careful, somebody is going to get hurt.

HALLY It won't be me.

SAM Don't be so sure.

HALLY I don't know what you're talking about, Sam.

SAM Yes, you do.

HALLY (*Furious*) Jesus, I wish you would stop trying to tell me what I do and what I don't know.

(SAM *gives up. He turns to* WILLIE)

SAM Let's finish up.

HALLY Don't turn your back on me! I haven't finished talking.

(*He grabs* SAM *by the arm and tries to make him turn around.* SAM *reacts with a flash of anger*)

SAM Don't do that, Hally! (*Facing the boy*) All right, I'm listening. Well? What do you want to say to me?

HALLY (*Pause as* HALLY *looks for something to say*) To begin with, why don't you also start calling me Master Harold, like Willie.

SAM Do you mean that?

HALLY Why the hell do you think I said it?

SAM And if I don't?

HALLY You might just lose your job.

SAM (*Quietly and very carefully*) If you make me say it once, I'll never call you anything else again.

HALLY So? (*The boy confronts the man*) Is that meant to be a threat?

SAM Just telling you what will happen if you make me do that. You must decide what it means to you.

HALLY Well, I have. It's good news. Because that is exactly what Master Harold wants from now on. Think of it as a little lesson in respect, Sam, that's long overdue, and I hope you remember it as well as you do your geography. I can tell you now that somebody who will be glad to hear I've finally given it to you will be my Dad. Yes! He agrees with my Mom. He's always going on about it as well. "You must teach the boys to show you more respect, my son."

SAM So now you can stop complaining about going home. Everybody is going to be happy tonight.

HALLY That's perfectly correct. You see, you mustn't get the wrong idea about me and my Dad, Sam. We also have our good times together. Some bloody good laughs. He's got a marvelous sense of humor. Want to know what our favorite joke is? He gives out a big groan, you see, and says: "It's not fair, is it, Hally?" Then I have to ask: "What, chum?" And then he says: "A nigger's arse" . . . and we both have a good laugh.

(*The men stare at him with disbelief*)

What's the matter, Willie? Don't you catch the joke? You always were a bit slow on the uptake. It's what is called a pun. You see, fair means both light in color and to be just and decent. (*He turns to* SAM) I thought *you* would catch it, Sam.

SAM Oh ja, I catch it all right.

HALLY But it doesn't appeal to your sense of humor.

SAM Do you really laugh?

HALLY Of course.

SAM To please him? Make him feel good?

HALLY No, for heaven's sake! I laugh because I think it's a bloody good joke.

SAM You're really trying hard to be ugly, aren't you? And why drag poor old Willie into it? He's done nothing to you except show you the respect you want so badly. That's also not being fair, you know . . . and *I* mean just or decent.

WILLIE It's all right, Sam. Leave it now.

SAM It's me you're after. You should just have said "Sam's arse" . . . because that's the one you're trying to kick. Anyway, how do you know it's not fair? You've never seen it. Do you want to? (*He drops his trousers and underpants and presents his backside for* HALLY'S *inspection*) Have a good look. A real Basuto arse . . . which is about as nigger as they can come. Satisfied? (*Trousers up*) Now you can make your Dad even happier when you go home tonight. Tell him I showed you my arse and he is quite right. It's not fair. And if it will give him an even better laugh next time, I'll also let *him* have a look. Come, Willie, let's finish up and go.

(SAM *and* WILLIE *start to tidy up the tea room.* HALLY *doesn't move. He waits for a moment when* SAM *passes him*)

HALLY (*Quietly*) Sam . . .

(SAM *stops and looks expectantly at the boy.* HALLY *spits in his face. A long and heartfelt groan from* WILLIE. *For a few seconds* SAM *doesn't move*)

SAM (*Taking out a handkerchief and wiping his face*) It's all right, Willie.

(*To* HALLY)

Ja, well, you've done it . . . Master Harold. Yes, I'll start calling you that from now on. It won't be difficult anymore. You've hurt yourself, Master Harold. I saw it coming. I warned you, but you wouldn't listen. You've just hurt yourself *bad*. And you're a coward, Master Harold. The face you should be spitting in is your father's . . . but you used mine, because you think you're safe inside your fair skin . . . and this time I don't mean just or decent. (*Pause, then moving violently towards* HALLY) Should I hit him, Willie?

WILLIE (*Stopping* SAM) No, Boet Sam.

SAM (*Violently*) Why not?

WILLIE It won't help, Boet Sam.

SAM I don't want to help! I want to hurt him.

WILLIE You also hurt yourself.

SAM And if he had done it to you, Willie?

WILLIE Me? Spit at me like I was a dog? (*A thought that had not occurred to him before. He looks at* HALLY) Ja. Then I want to hit him. I want to hit him hard!

(*A dangerous few seconds as the men stand staring at the boy.* WILLIE *turns away, shaking his head*)

But maybe all I do is go cry at the back. He's little boy, Boet Sam. Little *white* boy. Long trousers now, but he's still little boy.

SAM (*His violence ebbing away into defeat as quickly as it flooded*) You're right. So go on, then: groan again, Willie. You do it better than me. (*To* HALLY) You don't know all of what you've just done . . . Master Harold. It's not just that you've made me feel dirtier than I've ever been in my life . . . I mean, how do I wash off yours and your father's filth? . . . I've also failed. A long time ago I promised myself I was going to try and do something, but you've just shown me . . . Master Harold . . . that I've failed. (*Pause*) I've also got a memory of a little white boy when he was still wearing short trousers and a black man, but they're not flying a kite. It was the old Jubilee days, after dinner one night. I was in my room. You came in and just stood against the wall, looking down at the ground, and only after I'd asked you what you wanted, what was wrong, I don't know how many times, did you speak and even then so softly I almost didn't hear you. "Sam, please help me to go and fetch my Dad." Remember? He was dead drunk on the floor of the Central Hotel Bar. They'd phoned for your Mom, but you were the only one at home. And do you remember how we did it? You went in first by yourself to ask permission for me to go into the bar. Then I loaded him onto my back like a baby and carried him back to the boarding house with you following behind carrying his crutches. (*Shaking his head as he remembers*) A crowded Main Street with all the people watching a little white boy following his drunk father on a nigger's back! I felt for that little boy . . . Master Harold. I felt for him. After that we still had to clean him up, remember? He'd messed in his trousers, so we had to clean him up and get him into bed.

HALLY (*Great pain*) I love him, Sam.

SAM I know you do. That's why I tried to stop you from saying these things about him. It would have been so simple if you could have just despised him for being a weak man. But he's your father. You love him and you're ashamed of him. You're ashamed of so much! . . . And now that's going to include yourself. That was the promise I made to myself: to try and stop that happening. (*Pause*) After we got him to bed you came back with me to my room and sat in a corner and carried on just looking down at the ground. And for days after that! You hadn't done anything wrong, but you went around as if you owed the world an apology for being alive. I didn't like seeing that! That's not the way a boy grows up to be a man! . . . But the one person who should have been teaching you what that means was the cause of your shame. If you really want to know, that's why I made you that kite. I wanted you to look up, be proud of something, of yourself . . . (*Bitter smile at the memory*) . . . and you certainly were that when I left you with it up there on the hill. Oh, ja . . . something else! . . . If you ever do write it as a short story, there *was* a twist in our ending. I couldn't sit down there and stay with you. It was a "Whites Only" bench. You were too young, too excited to notice then. But not anymore. If you're not careful . . . Master Harold . . . you're going to be sitting up there by yourself for a long time to come, and there won't be a kite in the sky. (SAM *has got nothing more to say. He exits into the kitchen, taking off his waiter's jacket*)

WILLIE Is bad. Is all all bad in here now.

HALLY (*Books into his school case, raincoat on*) Willie . . . (*It is difficult to speak*) Will you lock up for me and look after the keys?

WILLIE Okay.

(SAM *returns.* HALLY *goes behind the counter and collects the few coins in the cash register. As he starts to leave* . . .)

SAM Don't forget the comic books.

(HALLY *returns to the counter and puts them in his case. He starts to leave again*)

SAM (*To the retreating back of the boy*) Stop . . . Hally . . .

(HALLY *stops, but doesn't turn to face him*)

Hally . . . I've got no right to tell you what being a man means if I don't behave like one myself, and I'm not doing so well at that this afternoon. Should we try again, Hally?

HALLY Try what?

SAM Fly another kite, I suppose. It worked once, and this time I need it as much as you do.

HALLY It's still raining, Sam. You can't fly kites on rainy days, remember.

SAM So what do we do? Hope for better weather tomorrow?

HALLY (*Helpless gesture*) I don't know. I don't know anything anymore.

SAM You sure of that, Hally? Because it would be pretty hopeless if that was true. It would mean nothing has been learnt in here this afternoon, and there was a hell of a lot of teaching going on . . . one way or the other. But anyway, I don't believe you. I reckon there's one thing you know. You don't *have* to sit up there by yourself. You know what that bench means now, and you can leave it any time you choose. All you've got to do is stand up and walk away from it.

(HALLY *leaves.* WILLIE *goes up quietly to* SAM)

WILLIE Is okay, Boet Sam. You see. Is . . . (*He can't find any better words*) . . . *is* going to be okay tomorrow. (*Changing his tone*) Hey, Boet Sam! (*He is trying hard*) You right. I think about it and you right. Tonight I find Hilda and say sorry. And make promise I won't beat her no more. You hear me, Boet Sam?

SAM I hear you, Willie.

WILLIE And when we practice I relax and romance with her from beginning to end. Non-stop! You watch! Two weeks' time: "First prize for promising newcomers: Mr. Willie Malopo and Miss Hilda Samuels." (*Sudden impulse*) To hell with it! I walk home. (*He goes to the jukebox, puts in a coin and selects a record. The machine comes to life in the gray twilight, blushing its way through a spectrum of soft, romantic colors*) How did you say it, Boet Sam? Let's dream. (WILLIE *sways with the music and gestures for* SAM *to dance*)

(*Sarah Vaughan sings*)

"Little man you're crying,
I know why you're blue,
Someone took your kiddy car away;
Better go to sleep now,
Little man you've had a busy day." (*etc. etc.*)

You lead. I follow.

(*The men dance together*)

"Johnny won your marbles,
Tell you what we'll do;
Dad will get you new ones
right away;
Better go to sleep now,
Little man you've had a
busy day."